롤러코스터
이래서 강력추천합니다!

체계적인 학습 | 초등학교 교육 과정을 충실히 반영하고 교과서 지문을 최대한 활용함으로써 학생들이 배워야 할 주요 학습 내용을 체계적으로 익힐 수 있도록 하였습니다.

학년별 맞춤 학습 | 모든 학년에서 표현과 낱말 학습을 기본으로 하되, 1·2학년은 Phonics, 3·4학년은 Reading & Writing, 5·6학년은 Grammar를 다루는 등, 각 학년별 주요 학습 영역을 중점적으로 다룸으로써 학년별 맞춤 학습을 추구하였습니다.

균형적인 학습 | 읽기, 쓰기 학습뿐만 아니라 오디오 CD와 동영상 CD를 활용한 듣기, 말하기 학습을 통해 영어의 4개 영역(Listening, Speaking, Reading, Writing)을 고루 마스터할 수 있도록 하였습니다.

자발적인 학습 | Song, Chant를 통해 표현을 자연스럽게 익히고, Cartoon을 통해 배운 내용을 재미있게 정리하는 등 다양한 Activity를 통해 학생들이 흥미를 가지고 적극적으로 수업에 참여할 수 있도록 하였습니다.

동영상을 통한 원어민과의 학습 | 원어민의 발음과 입모양을 동영상 CD를 통해 정확히 인지하고 학습자의 발음을 녹음해 원어민의 발음과 비교하여 들어 보게 함으로써 학습자 스스로 발음을 교정할 수 있는 기회를 제공하였습니다.

01 Student Book

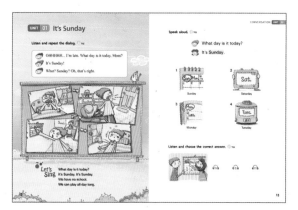

Conversation

초등영어 교과과정과 연계된 표현을
학습하고, 말하기 연습을 해본 다음,
다양한 확인 활동을 해봐요.

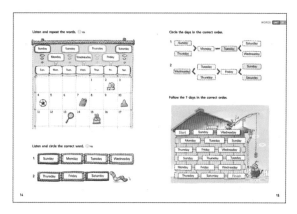

Words

생활 영어 표현과 관련된 낱말을 학습하고,
듣기, 읽기, 쓰기의 통합 활동을 통해
각 낱말을 익혀 봐요.

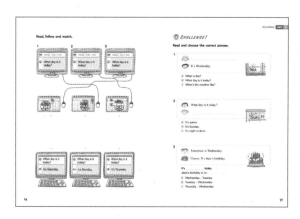

Reading

다양한 대화를 읽어 보며 표현에 대한
이해력을 높여 봐요.

Challenge : 각종 경시대회 및 TOEFL iBT에
대한 적응력을 높여주는 고난도 문제를
풀어 봐요.

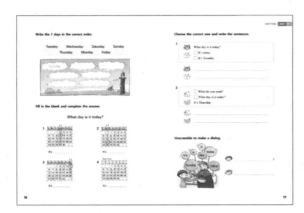

Writing

학습한 표현을 써 보면서, 자유롭게
활용할 수 있는 능력을 키워 봐요.

Cartoon

재미있는 만화를 통해 이미 학습한
표현과 낱말을 종합 정리해 봐요.

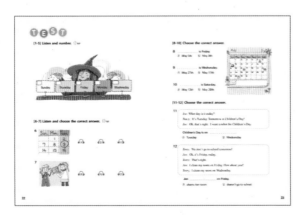

Test

테스트를 통해 학습한 표현 및 낱말에
대한 학습 성취도를 점검해 봐요.

02 Workbook

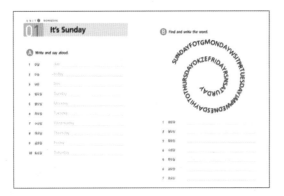

낱말을 따라 쓴 다음, 우리말에 해당하는 낱말을
직접 써 봐요.

표현을 따라 쓴 다음, 우리말에 해당하는 표현을
직접 써 봐요.

잘 듣고, 빈칸에 알맞은 낱말과
표현을 자신있게 써 봐요.

03 권말 테스트

낱말 및 표현에 관한 문제를 풀면서 그동안 쌓은
실력을 마음껏 발휘해 봐요.
(Achievement Test / Final Test)

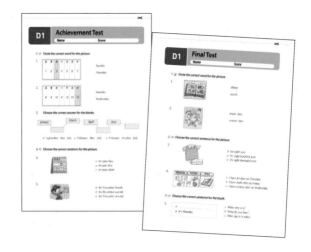

04 동영상 CD

Conversation

초등영어 교과과정과 연계된 표현을 배워 봐요.

Words

생활영어 표현과 관련된 낱말을 배워 봐요.

Speak

원어민의 발음과 입모양을 인지한 후,
직접 녹음해 봐요.

Song & Chant

즐겁게 노래하고 챈트하면서 학습한 내용을
정리해 봐요.

05 오디오 CD

Student Book, Workbook의 내용과 노래 및
챈트가 담겨 있어요.

Learning Points

D1

Unit Title	Theme	Function	Conversation
① It's Sunday	Days	· Talking about days	What day is it today? It's Sunday.
② It's June First	Dates	· Talking about dates	What's the date today? It's June first.
③ It's Two Thousand Won	Numbers	· Talking about price	How much is the watch? It's two thousand won.
④ I Have Art Class on Friday	Subjects	· Talking about subjects	I have Art class on Friday. Do you have Art class today? Yes, I do. No, I don't.

D2

Unit Title	Theme	Function	Conversation
① He Is Tall and Handsome	Adjectives	· Describing one's appearance	How does he look? He is tall and handsome.
② What a Big Building!	Adjectives	· Admiring	Look at the building! What a big building!
③ Whose Wallet Is This?	Possessive Adjectives	· Talking about possessions	Whose wallet is this? It's Jackie's wallet.
④ What's Your Favorite Vegetable?	Vegetables	· Expressing favorite vegetables	What's your favorite vegetable? I like carrots.

D3

Unit Title	Theme	Function	Conversation
① There Is a Bookcase in the Living Room	Rooms & Furniture	· Talking about location	Is there a bookcase in your bedroom? No, there isn't. There is a bookcase in the living room.
② Why Don't You Go Swimming?	Action Verbs	· Suggesting · Accepting and refusing	Why don't you go swimming? That's a good idea. / I don't want to.
③ Do You Need a Fork?	Kitchen Tools	· Talking about what someone needs	Do you need a fork? Yes, please. / No, that's OK. What do you need? I need a spoon.
④ What Time Do You Get up?	Daily Routine	· Expressing what someone does at a specific time	What time do you get up? I get up at 7 o'clock. What time do you go to school? I go to school at 8 o'clock.

D4

Unit Title	Theme	Function	Conversation
❶ I Have a Cold	Health	· Talking about common illnesses · Expressing concerns	Are you all right? No, I'm not. I have a cold. That's too bad.
❷ It's on the Bed	Prepositions	· Talking about prepositions	Where is my cap, Mom? It's on the bed. And... where is my bat? It's under the bed.
❸ She Is Wearing Jeans	Clothes	· Describing what one is wearing	What is she wearing? She's wearing a sweater and jeans. Is she wearing a muffler? Yes, she is.
❹ She Has Long Curly Hair	Adjectives	· Describing one's appearance	My sister has long curly hair. Do you have any sisters? Yes, I have one sister. She has short straight hair.

D5

Unit Title	Theme	Function	Conversation
❶ I Want to Ride a Bike	Action Verbs	· Expressing one's feelings · Talking about what one wants	What do you want to do? I want to ride a bike. I want to take a walk.
❷ It's Eight Thirty	Numbers	· Talking about the time	It's time for breakfast. What time is it? It's eight thirty.
❸ I'm Reading a Book	Action Verbs	· Describing what one is doing	What are you doing? I'm reading a book. I'm listening to music.
❹ There Are Two Hundred Cows on the Farm	Animals	· Counting	How many cows are there on the farm? There are two hundred cows on the farm.

D6

Unit Title	Theme	Function	Conversation
① Go Straight	Directions	· Talking about directions	Where is the subway station? Go straight. / Turn right. / Turn left.
② I'm Looking for a Tie for My Dad's Birthday	Clothes	· Expressing buying things at a store	May I help you? I'm looking for a tie for my dad's birthday. How about this one? That's nice.
③ I'm Going to the Post Office	Places	· Talking about one's destination	Where are you going? I'm going to the post office. / I'm going to the hair salon.
④ What Do You Usually Do After School?	Daily Routine	· Talking about daily activities	What do you usually do after school? I take ballet lessons. / I go inline skating.

Roller Coaster

Contents

UNIT 01 He Is Tall and Handsome

Listen and repeat the dialog. T02

Look! That's my teacher.

I can't see. How does he look?

He is tall and handsome.

🎵 Let's Sing

How does he look?
He is tall.
How does he look?
He is handsome.
He is tall and handsome.

Speak aloud. T03

 He (She) is tall .

1

short

2

handsome

3

pretty

4

fat

Listen and choose the correct answer.  T04

13

Listen and repeat the words. T05

handsome pretty tall short fat thin

Listen and write the number. T06

14

Circle the correct word.

1
fat

thin

2
tall

short

3
pretty

handsome

4
thin

fat

Circle the word and match it to the correct picture.

c d f a t o k s h o r t m i p r e t t y x k

Choose and write the correct number.

① She is tall.   ② He is thin.

③ She is fat.   ④ He is handsome.

⑤ She is pretty.   ⑥ He is short.

Read and connect the matching pairs.

1
> A: How does she look?
> B: She is tall and fat.

2
> A: How does she look?
> B: She is thin and pretty.

16

⭐ CHALLENGE!

Choose the correct answer.

1

 Look! That is my brother.

 I can't see. _____

 He is short and thin.

ⓐ How does she look?
ⓑ How does he look?
ⓒ Wow, he is handsome.

David   Sujie   Jack   Amy

2   **Which of the following is true for the picture?**

ⓐ David is fat, but he is handsome.
ⓑ Sujie is very tall and pretty.
ⓒ Jack is short and fat.

3   **Which of the following is NOT true for the picture?**

ⓐ Amy has short straight hair, and she is fat.
ⓑ Sujie is wearing a skirt, and she has curly hair.
ⓒ David is thin and he has short hair, and Jack has curly hair.

Write the correct word.

| David | Jenny | Sam | Betty | James | Meg |

fat   thin   tall

short   pretty   handsome

1 David is _____ handsome _____.

2 Jenny is _____.

3 Sam is _____.

4 Betty is _____.

5 James is _____.

6 Meg is _____.

Connect the matching pairs and write the correct sentence.

1   2   3

Danny   Jina   Chris

fat   thin   short   pretty   tall   handsome

1 <u>Danny is fat and short.</u>

2 _____

3 _____

Write the sentences to complete the dialog.

1

A: How does she look?

B: She is ___s___ and ___t___.

2

A: _____

B: _____

Guess Who?

Choose and complete the cartoon.

short (x2)   fat (x2)   How does he look?

[1-4] Listen and choose the correct picture. ◯ T07

1 ⓐ ⓑ 2 ⓐ ⓑ

3 ⓐ ⓑ 4 ⓐ ⓑ

[5-6] Listen and choose the correct answer. ◯ T08

5 ⓐ ⓑ ⓒ

6 ⓐ ⓑ ⓒ

[7-9] Choose the correct word for the blank.

7 He is tall _____ thin.
    ⓐ how   ⓑ and   ⓒ a

8 _____ does he look?
    ⓐ How   ⓑ Where   ⓒ Is

9 _____ is handsome.
    ⓐ I   ⓑ She   ⓒ He

10 Choose the correct dialog for the picture.

  ⓐ *A:* How does she look?
     B: She is short and fat.

  ⓑ *A:* How does he look?
     B: He is short and fat.

  ⓒ *A:* How does he look?
     B: He is tall and thin.

11 Choose the correct order to make a dialog.

A Oh, look! That is my sister.

B She is short and thin.

C I can't see. How does she look?

  ⓐ A－B－C
  ⓑ C－A－B
  ⓒ A－C－B

What a Big Building!

Listen and repeat the dialog. T09

Look at the building.

Wow! What a big building!

What's that?

That's a car.

What a big car!

Yes, it is a very big car.

Let's Chant

Big! Big!
Yes! Yes! It's a very big building.
Big! Big!
What a big car!
Yes! Yes! It's a very big car.

24

Speak aloud. T10

What a(an) big building !

1

delicious bread

2

small T-shirt

3

ugly dog

4

exciting game

Listen and choose the correct answer. T11

 ⓐ ⓑ

Listen and repeat the words. T12

big   small   ugly   delicious   exciting   wonderful

Listen and put a O or an X. T13

1   2   3

Connect the matching pairs.

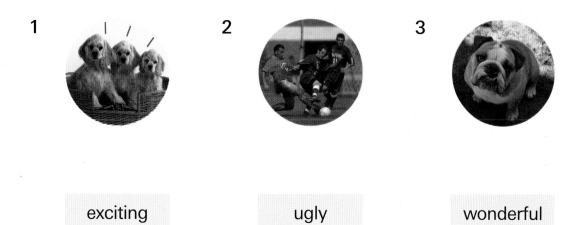

1

2

3

exciting

ugly

wonderful

Find the correct words and write the number.

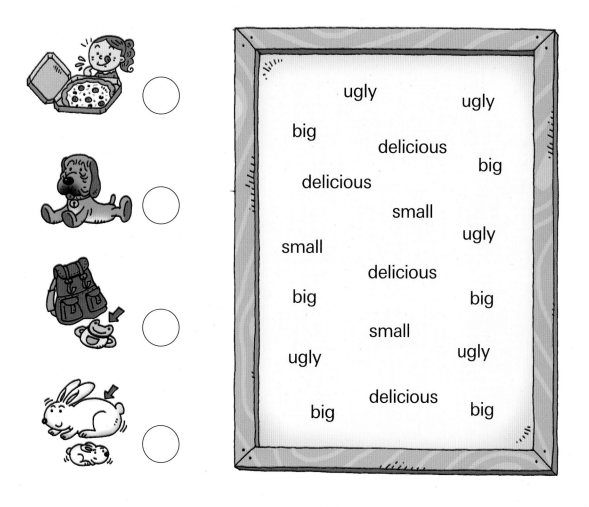

ugly   ugly

big
        delicious
                    big
delicious
            small
                ugly
small
        delicious
big   big
        small
ugly   ugly
        delicious
    big   big

Choose the correct sentence for the picture.

1
ⓐ It's a very big hat.

ⓑ What a small hat!

2
ⓐ What an exciting sport!

ⓑ It's a very delicious banana.

3
ⓐ It's a very pretty doll.

ⓑ What an ugly doll!

Connect the matching pairs.

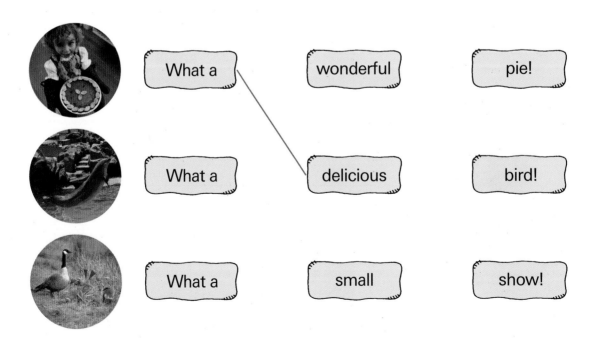

What a   wonderful   pie!

What a   delicious   bird!

What a   small   show!

⊙ CHALLENGE!

Choose the correct answer.

1

    _____

    Yes, it is.

    ⓐ What a wonderful boat!
    ⓑ What wonderful a boat!
    ⓒ What the wonderful boat!

A: There are two monkeys over there.

B: I see! One is very ugly.

A: Yes. _____(A)_____

B: Look over there. The dolphin show!

A: Wow! It's great!

B: Yes. _____(B)_____

2 **Which of the following is suitable for the blank (A)?**

    ⓐ What are they?
    ⓑ What an ugly monkey!
    ⓒ They are very ugly monkeys.

3 **Which of the following is NOT suitable for the blank (B)?**

    ⓐ It's a very wonderful show.
    ⓑ It's so boring.
    ⓒ What a wonderful show!

4 **Where are the speakers?**
  They are at the _____.

    ⓐ zoo   ⓑ farm   ⓒ supermarket

Write the words to complete the sentence.

1

_____ an _____ story!

2

_____ a _____ pizza!

3

_____ an _____ frog!

4

_____ a _____ cake!

delicious   exciting   What (x4)   big   ugly

Write the sentence using the given words.

1

wonderful / bike

_____

2

small / T-shirt

_____

Unscramble the words and write the sentence.

1 | small | what | cat | a | ! |

_____

2 a   what   movie   wonderful   !

_____

3 | bread | a | what | delicious | ! |

_____

Change the sentences using 'what'.

1
It is a very exciting game.

What an exciting game!

2
It is a very wonderful dress.

_____

3
It is a very big car.

_____

What a Poor Cindy!

Choose and complete the cartoon.

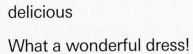

| delicious | big |
| What a wonderful dress! | What an ugly prince! |

What a _____ castle!

It is a very _____ cake.

Look!
The prince is coming.

Oh, no!
_____

[1-4] Listen and write the number. T14

 ☐

   ☐

 ☐

 ☐

[5-6] Listen and choose the correct picture. T15

5 ⓐ    ⓑ    ⓒ

6 ⓐ    ⓑ    ⓒ

7 Choose the one that is different from the others.

ⓐ short – tall   ⓑ big – small   ⓒ delicious – exciting

8 Choose the correct word for the blank.

It is a _____ ugly dog.

ⓐ very   ⓑ an   ⓒ much

[9-10] Choose the correct answer.

> A: Wow! It's a wonderful city.
>
> B: Look at the building.
>
> A: What a big building!
>
> B: Yes. Everything is _____ and wonderful in this city.
>
> A: I think so.

9 Which of the following is suitable for the blank?

ⓐ big   ⓑ small   ⓒ ugly

10 Which of the following is NOT true about the dialog?

ⓐ They are in the city.
ⓑ They don't like the big building.
ⓒ They think everything in the city is wonderful.

Listen and repeat the dialog. T16

 Whose wallet is this?

 It's Jackie's wallet.

 Jackie! Where is your wallet?

 Oh, no! Where is it?

 Here, Jackie. Be careful!

Let's Chant

Whose wallet?
Whose wallet is this?
Jackie's wallet.
It's Jackie's wallet.

Speak aloud. T17

 Whose wallet is this?

 It's Jackie's wallet .

1

Peter's / bike

2

Jane's / watch

3

Tom's / balloon

4

Kate's / teddy bear

Listen and choose the correct picture. T18

ⓐ

ⓑ

ⓒ

Listen and repeat the words. T19

| soccer ball | balloon | bike | wallet | watch | teddy bear |

Listen and write the number. T20

Circle the correct word.

1

watch

soccer ball

2

wallet

balloon

3

bike

balloon

4

ball

teddy bear

Fill in the blanks and find the picture.

te_ _y b_ _ _r   w_t_ _   _i_e   _o_ _er ba_ _

Whose things are they? Read and match.

1

A: Whose balloon is this?
B: It's Sean's balloon.

2

A: Whose soccer ball is this?
B: It's Terry's soccer ball.

3

A: Whose teddy bear is this?
B: It's Sonya's teddy bear.

4

A: Whose bike is this?
B: It's Sally's bike.

 **CHALLENGE!**

Choose the correct answer.

1

 It's Mary's teddy bear.

ⓐ Where is the teddy bear?
ⓑ Whose teddy bear is this?
ⓒ What is a teddy bear?

2

 Alice, is this Jane's wallet?

 No, it isn't.

 Then, whose wallet is this? Yours?

 No. It's _____.

ⓐ Jane's wallet
ⓑ Alice's wallet
ⓒ Susan's wallet

3 Which of the following is NOT true about the dialog?

 Oh, Susie. You're wearing a new watch.

 Yes, Joey. Do you like it?

 Yes. It looks great.

ⓐ Joey likes the new watch.
ⓑ The new watch looks great.
ⓒ Joey is wearing a new watch.

What are they? Write the correct words.

| teddy bear | watch | balloon | bike |

1 _____

2 _____

3 _____

4 _____

Trace and write.

1 Whose watch is this?

It's Will's watch.

2 Whose _____ is this?

It's _____ wallet.

Trace and complete the dialog.

Sean   Lena   Jay   Karen

1      Whose watch is this?

It's Karen's watch.

2   Whose _____ is this?

It's _____ soccer ball.

3      _____

_____

4      _____

_____

Be a Nice Friend!

Choose and complete the cartoon.

It's Brad's bike.   I'm sorry, Brad.   Whose bike is this?

[1-3] Listen and choose the correct picture. T21

1 ⓐ 　　ⓑ 　　ⓒ

2 ⓐ 　　ⓑ 　　ⓒ

3 ⓐ 　　ⓑ 　　ⓒ

[4-5] Listen and choose the correct answer. T22

4 Whose watch is it? 　ⓐ 　　ⓑ 　　ⓒ

5 Whose wallet is it? 　ⓐ 　　ⓑ 　　ⓒ

[6-7] Choose the correct answer.

6

It's Tim's _____.

ⓐ wallet   ⓑ teddy bear   ⓒ soccer ball

7

It's _____.

ⓐ Marians' balloon   ⓑ Marian balloon   ⓒ Marian's balloon

[8-9] Choose the correct answer.

> *Ian:* Whose bike is this?
> *Mandy:* It's Nick's bike.
> *Ian:* Wow! I love this bike. It's really cool.
> *Mandy:* I have a bike too. My bike is red.
> *Ian:* Really? I don't have a bike.

8 The red bike is _____ bike.

ⓐ Nick's   ⓑ Mandy's   ⓒ Ian's

9 Which of the following is NOT true about the dialog?

ⓐ Ian likes Nick's bike.
ⓑ Mandy doesn't like Nick's bike.
ⓒ Ian doesn't have a blike.

What's Your Favorite Vegetable?

Listen and repeat the dialog. 🔊 T23

> 👦 This vegetable soup is yummy.
>
> 👩 It's carrot soup.
>
> 👦 What's your favorite vegetable?
>
> 👩 I like carrots.

🎵 Let's Sing

What's your favorite vegetable?
What's your favorite vegetable?
Carrots! Carrots! I like carrots!
Carrots! Carrots! I like carrots!

Speak aloud. T24

 What's your favorite vegetable?

 I like carrots .

1

potatoes

2

cucumbers

3

tomatoes

4

onions

Listen and choose the correct answer. T25

 ⓐ   ⓑ   ⓒ

Listen and repeat the words. T26

| carrot | potato | onion | tomato | lettuce | cucumber |

Listen and choose the correct picture. T27

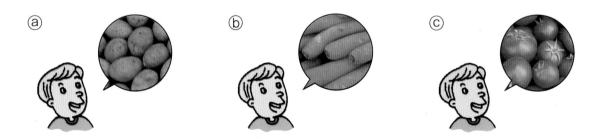

ⓐ   ⓑ   ⓒ

Draw a line to the correct picture.

tomato   lettuce   potato

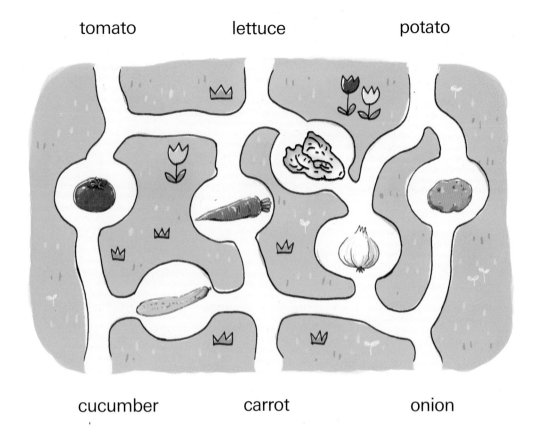

cucumber   carrot   onion

Circle the correct word.

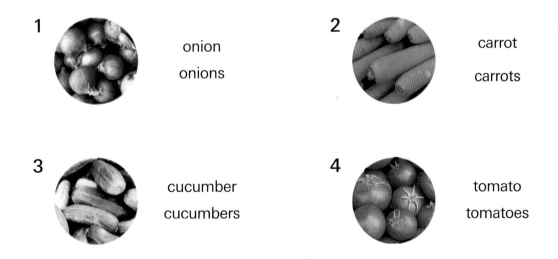

1 onion
   onions

2 carrot
   carrots

3 cucumber
   cucumbers

4 tomato
   tomatoes

Check True or False.

Tom	Jamie	Cathy	Jim

I like these.

1 Tom likes tomatoes.   ☐ True   ☐ False

2 Jamie likes cucumbers.   ☐ True   ☐ False

3 Cathy likes lettuce.   ☐ True   ☐ False

4 Jim likes potatoes.   ☐ True   ☐ False

Choose the correct answer.

1
What's your favorite vegetable?
I like onions.

ⓐ   ⓑ

2
What's your favorite vegetable?
I like lettuce.

ⓐ   ⓑ

 CHALLENGE!

1 Choose the correct answer.

 _____

 I like onions.

ⓐ What day is it today?
ⓑ What do you like doing?
ⓒ What's your favorite vegetable?

2 Who likes tomatoes?

Kelly: What's your favorite vegetable?

Peter: Tomatoes. What about you?

Kelly: I like tomatoes too.

ⓐ Kelly.　　　　ⓑ Peter.　　　　ⓒ Kelly and Peter.

3 Which of the following is true about the passage?

Hello, I'm Tim. Let me tell you about
my family's favorite vegetables.
My sister likes tomatoes.
My mom likes lettuce. My dad likes it too.
My favorite vegetables are cucumbers.
What about you?

ⓐ Tim likes onions.
ⓑ Tim's dad likes lettuce.
ⓒ Tim's sister likes cucumbers.

Find and write the word.

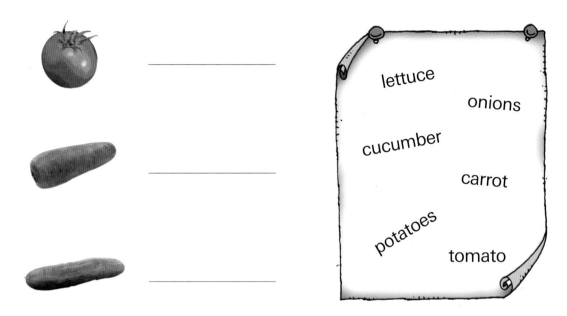

Complete the answer to the question.

Q: What's your favorite vegetable?

1 I like _____ .

2 I _____ .

3 _____ .

Unscramble and write the sentence.

1

vegetable   your   favorite   what's   ?

_____

2

like   .   I   tomatoes

_____

3

I   onions   .   like

_____

Order the sentences to make a dialog.

I like carrots.

What's your favorite vegetable?

I like them too.

 _____

 _____

 _____

I Can Help Myself

Choose and complete the cartoon.

I like potatoes.

I like carrots.

Here you are.

What's your favorite vegetable?

[1-6] Listen and write the number. T28

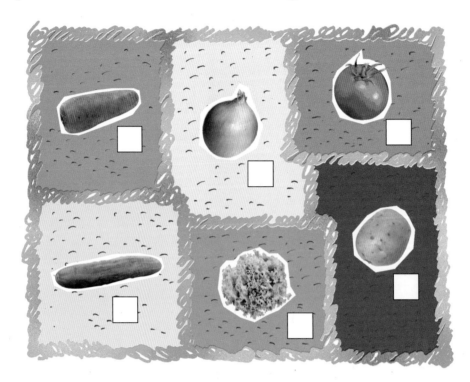

[7-8] Listen and choose the correct answer. T29

7

ⓐ   ⓑ   ⓒ

8

ⓐ   ⓑ   ⓒ

[9-12] Circle the correct word.

9

carrot

onion

10

letter

lettuce

11

fruit

vegetable

12

tomato

potato

[13-14] Choose the correct answer.

13 I like potatoes.

ⓐ ⓑ ⓒ

14 *A:* What's your favorite vegetable?
B: I like cucumbers.

ⓐ ⓑ ⓒ

Game

Guess Who!

Mark

Jane

David

Mat

Mary

Chris

Lisa

Jenny

Word Box
tall
short
fat
thin

❶ 두 명이 짝이 되어 하는 게임으로 가위바위보를 하여 진 사람(학생 A라 가정)이 그림 속의 한 인물을 정하면
  이긴 사람(학생 B)이 그 인물의 생김새를 물어 보고, 진 사람이 그 인물에 대해 설명하세요.
  설명할 때 Word Box에 있는 낱말을 사용하세요.
  ex) A: This is a boy〔girl〕.
      B: How does he〔she〕look?
      A: He〔She〕is fat.
❷ 이긴 사람(학생 B)이 그림 속에서 해당 인물을 맞히세요. *ex)* He〔She〕is David〔Jane〕.
❸ 맞히면 1점을 얻고, 틀리면 상대방에게 기회가 넘어가게 돼요.
❹ 더 많은 점수를 얻는 사람이 이기는 게임이에요.

Round and Round the World

준비물 : 주사위, 마커

❶ 게임을 시작하기 전에 선생님과 함께 보드판에 쓰여 있는 낱말을 확인해 보세요.

❷ 학생 두 명이 각자 자신이 원하는 START 위치에 마커를 놓고 주사위를 던진 다음, 해당 칸으로 마커를 이동하세요.

❸ 해당 그림 아래의 명사와 가운데의 형용사를 알맞게 사용하여 "What a(n) _____ _____!"라고 말하세요.
맞게 대답하면 그 칸에 멈추고 틀리면 이전의 자리로 돌아가세요.

❹ 'Miss a Turn' 칸에 도착하면 순서를 한 번 잃게 되고 'Go Back' 칸에 도착하면 이전의 자리로 돌아가게 돼요.

❺ 자신이 시작한 위치로 먼저 돌아오는 사람이 이기는 게임이에요.

Turtle Race

START

① Peter

② ③ ④ ⑤ ⑥ ⑦ ⑧ ⑨ ⑩

Sally

Jane

Tom

John

Amy

Jake

Anna

FINISH

준비물 : 동전, 마커

❶ 두 명이 각자의 마커를 START에 놓고 한 학생(학생 A라 가정)이 동전을 던져 앞면이 나오면 두 칸, 뒷면이 나오면 한 칸을 이동하세요.

❷ 해당 칸에 도착하면 상대방(학생 B)이 해당 사물 이름을 넣어 "Whose (wallet) is this?"라고 질문하면, 학생 A는 사물 옆 또는 아래에 쓰여 있는 사람의 이름과 사물 이름을 넣어 "It's (Peter)'s (wallet)."이라고 대답하세요.

❸ 맞게 대답하면 이동한 칸에 멈추고 틀리면 이전의 자리로 되돌아가요. 폭탄을 만나면 한 칸 뒤로 이동해야 해요.

❹ 먼저 FINISH에 도착하는 사람이 이기는 게임이에요.

Concentration Game

Cut out and play.

준비물 : 가위

❶ 두 명이 짝이 되어 각자의 카드를 자르고 두 세트의 카드를 섞으세요.

❷ 모두 뒤집어서 배열한 후에 가위바위보로 순서를 정하세요.

❸ 이긴 학생(학생 A라 가정)이 카드를 뒤집기 전에 상대방(학생 B)이 "What's your favorite vegetable?"이라고 질문하면 학생 A는 카드를 뒤집은 다음, 야채 이름을 넣어 "I like _____."라고 대답하세요.

❹ 같은 방법으로 한 장의 카드를 더 뒤집어서 두 개의 카드 그림이 같으면 학생 A는 그 두 장의 카드를 가질 수 있어요. 같은 카드 두 장을 뒤집은 학생 A는 카드를 뒤집을 기회를 한 번 더 가지게 돼요.

❺ 더 많은 카드를 가진 학생이 이기는 게임이에요.

Roller Coaster D2
Student Book

UNIT 01

P. 13

ⓐ She is tall.
ⓑ He is tall.
ⓒ He is short.

P. 14

1 thin   2 short   3 pretty

P. 15

 fat / thin

 tall / short

pretty / handsome

thin / fat

 c d f a t o k s h o r t m i p r e t t y x k

P. 16

④ ⑥ ⑤ ① ③ ②

1 A: How does she look?
B: She is tall and fat.

2 A: How does she look?
B: She is thin and pretty.

P. 17

1 ⓑ   2 ⓒ   3 ⓐ

P. 18

2 Jenny is pretty.   3 Sam is thin.
4 Betty is fat.   5 James is short.
6 Meg is tall.

P. 19

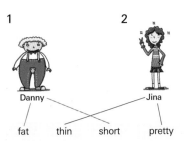
Danny   Jina   Chris
fat thin short pretty tall handsome

2 Jina is thin and pretty.
3 Chris is tall and handsome.

1 *B:* She is short and thin.

2 *A:* How does he look?

  B: He is tall〔handsome〕and handsome〔tall〕.

P. 20-21

CARTOON

How does he look?

Hmm, he is short〔fat〕and fat〔short〕!

Jim is short〔fat〕and fat〔short〕.

P. 22-23

TEST

🎧 1 tall	2 thin	3 short	4 fat

1 ⓐ   2 ⓑ   3 ⓐ   4 ⓐ

🎧 5 ⓐ He is fat.
    ⓑ He is thin.
    ⓒ She is tall.

   6 ⓐ She is short and fat.
    ⓑ She is tall and thin.
    ⓒ She is fat and pretty.

5 ⓐ   6 ⓑ

7 ⓑ   8 ⓐ   9 ⓒ   10 ⓒ   11 ⓒ

UNIT 02

P. 25

🎧 ⓐ It's a very small shoe.
   ⓑ What a big shoe!

P. 26

🎧 1 delicious	2 exciting	3 big

P. 27

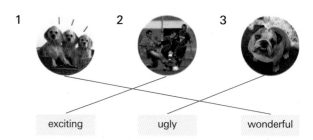

exciting   ugly   wonderful

P. 28

1 ⓐ   2 ⓑ   3 ⓑ

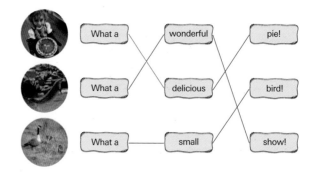

P. 29

1 ⓐ   2 ⓑ   3 ⓑ   4 ⓐ

P. 30

1 <u>What</u> an <u>exciting</u> story!
2 <u>What</u> a <u>delicious</u> pizza!
3 <u>What</u> an <u>ugly</u> frog!
4 <u>What</u> a <u>big</u> cake!

1 What a wonderful bike!
2 What a small T-shirt!

P. 31

1 What a small cat!
2 What a wonderful movie!
3 What a delicious bread!

2 What a wonderful dress!
3 What a big car!

P. 32-33

CARTOON
What a wonderful dress!
What a <u>big</u> castle!
It is a very <u>delicious</u> cake.
What an ugly prince!

P. 34-35

TEST

 1 delicious   2 exciting
      3 wonderful   4 big

5 *A:* What a small bird!
   B: Yes, it is.

6 *A:* It's a very exciting movie.
   B: Yes, it is.

5 ⓐ   6 ⓑ

7 ⓒ   8 ⓐ   9 ⓐ   10 ⓑ

UNIT 03

P. 37

A: Whose watch is this?
B: It's John's watch.

P. 38

1 soccer ball   2 teddy bear   3 balloon

 2   3   1

P. 39

1   watch
   soccer ball

2   wallet
   balloon

3   bike
   balloon

4   ball
    teddy bear

67

te<u>d</u>dy b<u>e</u>a<u>r</u>   w<u>a</u>t<u>c</u>h   b<u>i</u>ke   <u>s</u>o<u>c c</u>er ba<u>l</u>l

P. 40

Terry   Sally   Sonya   Sean

P. 41

1 ⓑ   2 ⓒ   3 ⓒ

P. 42

1 bike   2 teddy bear
3 watch   4 balloon

2 Whose <u>wallet</u> is this?

     It's <u>Jane's</u> wallet.

P. 43

2 Whose <u>soccer ball</u> is this?
   It's <u>Sean's</u> soccer ball.

3 Whose balloon is this?
   It's Jay's balloon.

4 Whose bike is this?
   It's Lena's bike.

P. 44-45

CARTOON
Whose bike is this?
It's Brad's bike.
I'm sorry, Brad.

P. 46 -47

TEST

| 🎧 1 teddy bear | 2 soccer ball | 3 bike |

1 ⓑ   2 ⓒ   3 ⓐ

🎧 4 ⓐ It's Andy's watch.
       ⓑ It's Ann's watch.
       ⓒ It's Cathy's watch.

    5 ⓐ It's Brian's wallet.
       ⓑ It's Cathy's wallet.
       ⓒ It's Andy's wallet.

4 ⓐ   5 ⓑ

6 ⓒ   7 ⓒ   8 ⓑ   9 ⓑ

UNIT 04

P. 49

ⓐ *A:* What's your name?
B: My name is Julie.

ⓑ *A:* Do you want some cookies?
B: Yes, please.

ⓒ *A:* What's your favorite vegetable?
B: I like potatoes.

P. 50

I like carrots.

ⓐ    ⓑ   ⓒ

P. 51

tomato   lettuce   potato

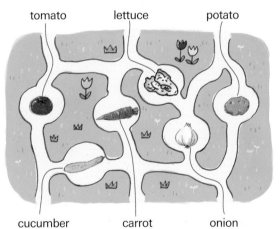

cucumber   carrot   onion

1 onion
(onions)

2 carrot
(carrots)

3 cucumber
(cucumbers)

4 tomato
(tomatoes)

P. 52

	Tom	Jamie	Cathy	Jim
I like these.				

		True	False
1	Tom likes tomatoes.	☑ True	☐ False
2	Jamie likes cucumbers.	☐ True	☑ False
3	Cathy likes lettuce.	☐ True	☑ False
4	Jim likes potatoes.	☑ True	☐ False

1 ⓐ   ⓑ

2 ⓐ   ⓑ

P. 53

1 ⓒ   2 ⓒ   3 ⓑ

P. 54

 tomato

 carrot

 cucumber

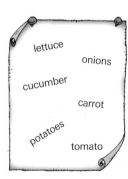

lettuce
onions
cucumber
carrot
potatoes
tomato

1 I like lettuce.

2 I like onions.

3 I like potatoes.

P. 55

1 What's your favorite vegetable?

2 I like tomatoes.

3 I like onions.

  What's your favorite vegetable?

  I like carrots.

  I like them too.

P. 56-57

CARTOON
I like carrots.
What's your favorite vegetable?
I like potatoes.
Here you are.

P. 58-59

TEST

1 lettuce	2 cucumber	3 carrot
4 potato	5 onion	6 tomato

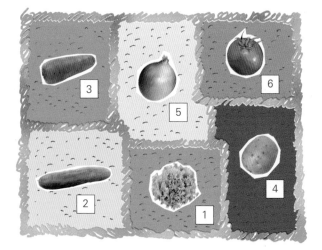

7 ⓐ I like lettuce.
   ⓑ I like carrots.
   ⓒ I like cucumbers.

8 ⓐ *A:* What color is it?
      B: It's blue.

   ⓑ *A:* Do you want some ice cream?
      B: Yes, please.

   ⓒ *A:* What's your favorite vegetable?
      B: I like onions.

7 ⓐ   8 ⓒ

9   carrot
                           onion

10   letter
                            lettuce

11   fruit
                            vegetable

12   tomato
                            potato

13 ⓐ   14 ⓒ

Roller Coaster D2
Workbook

UNIT 01

P. 2

1 tall	2 pretty	3 fat
4 thin	5 short	6 handsome
7 and	8 how	9 she

P. 5

🎧 1 pretty	2 fat	3 short
4 handsome	5 tall	6 thin

🎧 I Look! That's my friend.
① How does she look?
She is ② short and pretty.

II Do you see the boy over there?
No. ③ How does he look?
④ He is tall and thin.

UNIT 02

P. 7

Across (→)
1 큰 big
2 멋진 wonderful

Down (↓)
3 재미있는 exciting
4 맛있는 delicious
5 못생긴 ugly

P. 10

🎧 1 wonderful	2 small	3 ugly
4 big	5 delicious	6 exciting

🎧 I It's a very ① delicious cake.
Yes, it is. ② What a delicious cake!

II What's that?
That's a car.
③ What a big car!
Yes, it is a ④ very big car.

UNIT 03

P. 12

1 지갑	wallet
2 손목 시계	watch
3 풍선	balloon
4 축구공	soccer ball
5 자전거	bike
6 테디 베어	teddy bear

P. 15

🎧 1 soccer ball	2 bike	3 balloon
4 watch	5 teddy bear	6 wallet

🎧 I Whose ① watch is this?
It's ② John's watch.

II ③ Whose wallet is this?
It's ④ Jackie's wallet.
Jackie! ⑤ Where is your wallet?
Oh, no. Where is it?
Here, Jackie. Be careful!

UNIT 04

P. 17

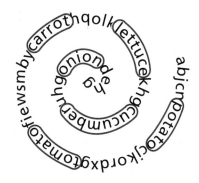

1	당근	carrot
2	오이	cucumber
3	토마토	tomato
4	양상추	lettuce
5	감자	potato
6	양파	onion

P. 20

🎧 1 tomato   2 cucumber   3 lettuce
   4 onion   5 carrot   6 potato

🎧 I This vegetable soup is ① yummy.
What's your ② favorite vegetable?
I ③ like carrots.

II ④ What's your favorite vegetable?
⑤ I like onions.

Test

Achievement Test

🎧 1 ⓐ tall   ⓑ short   ⓒ fat
   2 ⓐ delicious   ⓑ ugly   ⓒ exciting

1 ⓐ   2 ⓒ

🎧 3 She is thin and pretty.
   4 What an ugly doll!

3 ⓑ   4 ⓐ

5 ⓒ   6 ⓑ   7 ⓑ

8 ⓐ   9 ⓒ   10 ⓒ

Final Test

🎧 1 wallet   2 lettuce

1 ⓑ   2 ⓐ

🎧 3 ⓐ It's Karen's watch.
     ⓑ It's Sally's watch.
     ⓒ It's Karen's bike.
   4 ⓐ I like onions.
     ⓑ I like cucumbers.
     ⓒ I like carrots.

3 ⓐ   4 ⓒ

5 ⓐ   6 ⓑ   7 ⓑ

8 ⓒ   9 ⓐ   10 ⓑ

01 He Is Tall and Handsome

A Write and say aloud.

1	잘생긴	handsome
2	예쁜	pretty
3	키가 큰	tall
4	키가 작은	short
5	뚱뚱한	fat
6	마른	thin
7	그	he
8	그녀	she
9	어떻게	how
10	그리고	and

1

B Unscramble the letters.

1 키가 큰   latl   _____

2 예쁜   yrptet   _____

3 뚱뚱한   fta   _____

4 마른   hint   _____

5 키가 작은   oshtr   _____

6 잘생긴   moseahnd _____

7 그리고   dna   _____

8 어떻게   owh   _____

9 그녀   esh   _____

C Write and say aloud.

1 그는 어떻게 생겼니?

   How does he look?

2 그는 잘생겼어.

   He is handsome.

3 그는 키가 커.

   He is tall.

4 그녀는 키가 작아.

   She is short.

5 그녀는 말랐어.

   She is thin.

6 그녀는 예뻐.

She is pretty.
_____

_____

7 그녀는 키가 크고 뚱뚱해.

She is tall and fat.
_____

_____

8 그는 키가 작고 말랐어.

He is short and thin.
_____

_____

9 저 분이 나의 선생님이셔.

That's my teacher.
_____

_____

10 나는 볼 수가 없어. 〔나는 안 보이는데.〕

I can't see.
_____

_____

D   Listen and write the word. 🎧 ⊙ T30

1 _____

2 _____

3 _____

4 _____

5 _____

6 _____

E   Listen and fill in the blanks. 🎧 ⊙ T31

Ⅰ   Look! That's my friend.

① _____ does she _____?

She is ② _____ and _____.

Ⅱ   Do you see the boy over there?

No. ③ _____

④ _____

02

What a Big Building!

A Write and say aloud.

1	큰	big
2	작은	small
3	멋진	wonderful
4	못생긴	ugly
5	재미있는	exciting
6	맛있는	delicious
7	빵	bread
8	원숭이	monkey
9	자동차	car
10	티셔츠	T-shirt

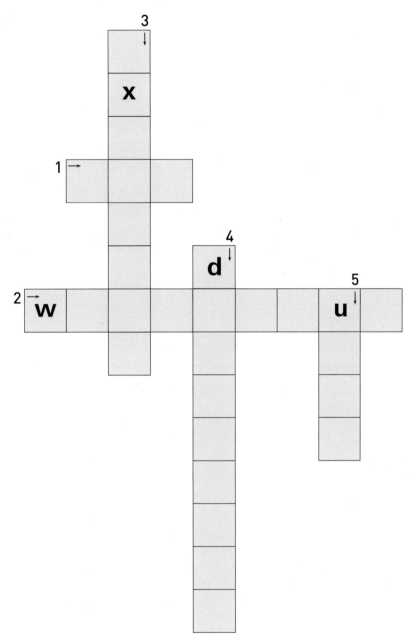

Across(→)

1 큰

2 멋진

Down(↓)

3 재미있는

4 맛있는

5 못생긴

C Write and say aloud.

1 건물을 봐.

Look at the building.

2 정말 큰 건물이야!

What a big building!

3 그것은 정말 큰 자동차야.

It is a very big car.

4 그것은 정말 큰 모자야.

It's a very big hat.

5 정말 큰 도시야!

What a big city!

6 정말 못생긴 인형이야!

What an ugly doll!

_____

_____

7 정말 재미있는 이야기야!

What an exciting story!

_____

_____

8 정말 큰 개야!

What a big dog!

_____

_____

9 정말 멋진 자전거야!

What a wonderful bike!

_____

_____

10 정말 맛있는 파이야!

What a delicious pie!

_____

_____

D Listen and write the word. 🎧 💿 T32

1 _____

2 _____

3 _____

4 _____

5 _____

6 _____

E Listen and fill in the blanks. 🎧 💿 T33

I It's a very ① _____ cake.

Yes, it is. ② _____ cake!

II What's that?

That's a car.

③ _____

Yes, it is a ④ _____ .

03 Whose Wallet Is This?

A Write and say aloud.

1 축구공   soccer ball

2 자전거   bike

3 풍선   balloon

4 손목 시계   watch

5 테디 베어   teddy bear

6 지갑   wallet

7 누구의   whose

8 재키의   Jackie's

9 어디   where

Find and write the word.

c	w	a	l	l	e	t	n	e	l	b
t	e	d	d	y		b	e	a	r	t
w	s	t	h	r	i	b	t	o	b	r
a	z	k	a	n	a	t	u	t	i	q
t	r	b	a	l	l	o	o	n	k	x
c	c	t	e	c	o	a	i	t	e	z
h	m	g	e	q	r	p	f	o	o	s
r	e	f	a	o	v	r	i	e	t	m
s	o	c	c	e	r		b	a	l	l

1 지갑   _____

2 손목 시계   _____

3 풍선   _____

4 축구공   _____

5 자전거   _____

6 테디 베어   _____

12

C Write and say aloud.

1 이것은 누구의 지갑이니?

Whose wallet is this?

2 그것은 재키의 지갑이야.

It's Jackie's wallet.

3 네 지갑은 어디에 있니?

Where is your wallet?

4 조심해!

Be careful!

5 이것은 누구의 테디 베어니?

Whose teddy bear is this?

6 그것은 케이트의 테디 베어야.

It's Kate's teddy bear.
_____

_____

7 이것은 누구의 자전거니?

Whose bike is this?
_____

_____

8 그것은 존의 자전거야.

It's John's bike.
_____

_____

9 이것은 누구의 시계니?

Whose watch is this?
_____

_____

10 그것은 메리의 손목 시계야.

It's Mary's watch.
_____

_____

D Listen and write the word. 🎧 💿 T34

1 _____

2 _____

3 _____

4 _____

5 _____

6 _____

E Listen and fill in the blanks. 🎧 💿 T35

I Whose ① _____ is _____?

It's ② _____ .

II ③ _____ _____ is this?

It's ④ _____ .

Jackie! ⑤ _____ ?

Oh, no. Where is it?

Here, Jackie. Be careful!

04 What's Your Favorite Vegetable?

A Write and say aloud.

1 야채   vegetable

2 당근   carrot

3 오이   cucumber

4 감자   potato

5 양파   onion

6 토마토   tomato

7 양상추   lettuce

8 가장 좋아하는   favorite

9 좋아하다   like

10 맛있는   yummy

B Find and write the word.

abjcnpotatocjkordxgtomatofjewsmbycarrothqolklettucekhgcucumberhgoniondefg

1 당근   _carrot_

2 오이   _cucumber_

3 토마토   _tomato_

4 양상추   _lettuce_

5 감자   _potato_

6 양파   _onion_

C Write and say aloud.

1 이 야채 수프는 맛있어.

This vegetable soup is yummy.

2 가장 좋아하는 야채가 뭐니?

What is your favorite vegetable?

3 나는 양파를 좋아해.

I like onions.

4 나는 감자를 좋아해.

I like potatoes.

5 내가 가장 좋아하는 야채는 양상추야.

My favorite vegetable is lettuce.

6 누가 토마토를 좋아하니?

Who likes tomatoes?

_____

7 짐은 토마토를 좋아해.

Jim likes tomatoes.

_____

8 톰은 당근을 좋아해.

Tom likes carrots.

_____

9 우리 엄마는 양상추를 좋아하셔.

My mom likes lettuce.

_____

10 나의 오빠는 양파를 좋아해.

My brother likes onions.

_____

1 _____

2 _____

3 _____

4 _____

5 _____

6 _____

E   Listen and fill in the blanks. 🎧 💿 T37

Ⅰ   This vegetable soup is ① _____ .

    What's your ② _____ vegetable?

    I ③ _____ _____ .

Ⅱ   ④ _____

    ⑤ _____